BMW

W
FRANKLIN WATTS
LONDON·SYDNEY

This paperback edition
first published in 2007 by
Franklin Watts
338 Euston Road
London NW1 3BH

Franklin Watts Australia
Hachette Children's Books
Level 17/207 Kent Street
Sydney NSW 2000

ISBN 978 0 7496 7243 0

© 2005 The Brown Reference Group plc

A CIP catalogue record for this book is available
from the British Library

Printed in China

For The Brown Reference Group plc

Editor: Bridget Giles
Managing Editor: Tim Cooke
Design Manager: Lynne Ross
Children's Publisher: Anne O'Daly
Production Director: Alastair Gourlay
Editorial Director: Lindsey Lowe

Credits
Pictures: IMP AB
Text: The Brown Reference Group plc/
IMP AB

Some words are shown in **bold**, like this.

You can find out what they mean by looking

at the bottom right of most right-hand pages.

You can also find most of the words in the

Glossary on page 30.

Contents

Introduction	4
BMW 3 Series	6
BMW 325i Cabriolet	10
BMW 5 Series	14
BMW 750i	18
BMW Z3	22
BMW M Series	26

Glossary	30
Further Information	31
Index	32

Introduction

In 1916 two German companies that made engines for airplanes joined to form Bayerische Motoren Werke (Bavarian Motor Works, or BMW). In 1923 the company began making motorcycles. Based on the success of these motorcycles, BMW started producing cars in 1928. The company grew in popularity until World War II (1939–1945). During the war BMW's factories were destroyed by bombs. After the

The design of BMW's badge is based on a plane's spinning propeller.

The M1 was introduced in the late 1970s. It was BMW's first model in the powerful and upmarket Motorsport range.

war the company was near ruin and had to rely on its motorcycles to keep from going bankrupt. Then, in the late 1960s, BMW began making four-seat saloons and smaller coupés that performed like sports cars. From the early 1970s to the late 1990s, BMW enjoyed success with the 3 Series, 325i Cabriolet convertible, 5 Series, 750i, Z3 and M Series — each a modern classic.

The 750i is BMW's top-of-the-range luxury saloon. The model was introduced in the late 1980s. It is still one of the most sophisticated cars available.

On the outside the M Roadster looks similar to the Z3. On the inside, however, the M Series engine makes the M Roadster one of the most powerful sports cars.

BMW 3 Series

With top speeds of around 228 km/h (142 mph) and with a high-performance, six-cylinder engine, the BMW 3 Series of the late 1990s was one of the most powerful and fastest mid-to-top-range cars on the road. In head-to-head tests the 3 Series 323i is faster than rivals like the Mazda Millennia and the Audi A4 2.8 Quattro. The 3 Series 323i also has better steering control and grips the road tighter than a 1968–1975 BMW model, the 2002 coupé.

Vital Statistics for the 1998 BMW 323i

Top speed:	*228.5 km/h (142 mph)*
0–60 mph:	*7.9 seconds*
Engine:	*In-line six*
Engine size:	*2,494 cc (152.2 ci)*
Power:	*170 bhp at 5,500 rpm*
Weight:	*1,430 kg (3,153 lb)*
Fuel economy:	*26 mpg*

The interior of the top-range, 3-Series models has stylish leather seats and wood trim.

Milestones

1975

BMW introduces the 3 Series as a large, box-shaped model to replace the 2002 coupé.

1982

BMW revises the 3 Series with a smoother body and begins making the M3.

1990

The new 3 Series is bigger, heavier and has a more angular shape than before.

1998

The fourth generation of the 3 Series appears. Models include 318i and a new 323i.

"In the new BMW 3 Series ... acceleration from the straight-six engine is ... superb, the massive disc brakes are simply amazing, and it's a truly refined package."

In 1982 BMW introduced the first **convertible** to the 3 Series. The 1982 model was so popular that the design remained more or less the same until 2001. The new version of the convertible is another high-profile model of the 3 Series.

Convertible   A type of car with a top that can be lowered or removed.

Specifications

Formerly thought of as BMW's junior sports **saloon**, the 3 Series is now an upmarket car, well suited for either a small family or a sports driver. New developments, such as a six-cylinder engine, make it one of the most advanced cars on the road.

Six-cylinder engine
The six-cylinder engine, engineered to give the optimum smoothness when running, is standard in both the 323i and 328i models.

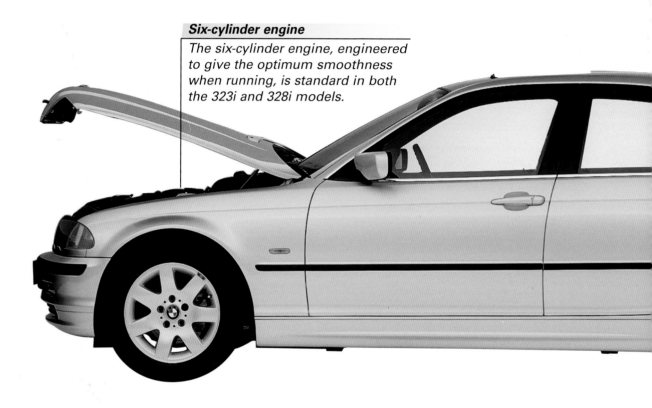

Hot key memory system
A key-and-car memory system allows the driver to preset the seat position and air-conditioning level. Each time the driver uses his or her own key, the car adjusts to the chosen settings.

 The rear suspension is known as 'multi-link'. It includes coil springs, telescopic shock absorbers and an anti-roll bar for a smoother, safer ride.

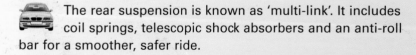 The current 3 Series, like its sports saloon predecessor, has a five-speed manual **transmission**.

Optional infrared windscreen

An optional infrared windscreen is available. It reflects direct sunlight and stops the surface of the instrument panel getting too hot.

Bumper sensors

An echo sounder and sensors in the rear bumper signal the driver that the car is too close to other cars or objects. This lessens the risk of scrapes and scratches.

Saloon	A car with two or four doors and seats for four or more people.
Transmission	Speed-changing gears and other parts that transmit power from engine to wheels.

BMW 325i Cabriole

The 325i Cabriolet convertible was a revolutionary car for BMW in the 1980s. A modern classic, the 325i Cabriolet had the performance of a sports car, such as responsive handling and excellent **roadholding**. It also had the comfort and security of a fixed-roof car. The 325i Cabriolet was faster than either the Audi Cabriolet or the Saab 900 Turbo Convertible of the same era. It set the standard for upmarket **coupé** convertibles.

Vital Statistics for the 1990 BMW 325i

Top speed:	*209 km/h (130 mph)*
0–60 mph:	*7.5 seconds*
Engine:	*In-line six*
Engine size:	*2,494 cc (152.2 ci)*
Power:	*168 bhp at 5,800 rpm*
Weight:	*1,355 kg (2,988 lb)*
Fuel economy:	*25 mpg*

The leather interior in the 325i is both stylish and practical. Leather is easier to wipe down if the convertible is caught in the rain with its roof down.

Milestones

1982
BMW launches the 323i, a new 3 Series car. It has a wider base for extra stability.

1985
BMW replaces the 323i with the new 325i. The engine is larger, with more horsepower.

1986
The first 325i convertible is introduced by BMW. It has a strengthened windscreen.

1993
At the Geneva international car show, BMW launches a brand new 325i.

"*Despite the 325i Cabriolet being more than 90 kg (200 lb) heavier than the fixed-head version, performance does not suffer. The car can sprint to 160 km/h (100 mph) in 22 seconds.*"

In the early 1980s BMW introduced a convertible to the 3 Series. The body of the new car had reinforced steel throughout. It was particularly strong around the windscreen. The frame would not buckle if the car rolled over. It would protect the occupants. When the 325i Cabriolet was produced it too had a strengthened body. It was one of the safest convertibles of the time.

Coupé	A two-door car that usually seats four people.
Roadholding	A car's ability to grip the road without sliding.

11

Specifications

Introducing the 325i Cabriolet into the 3 Series in the early 1980s gave BMW one of the most popular sports convertibles of the decade. The 325i Cabriolet was one of the sleekest-looking convertibles on the road. It was also one of the safest.

Rev limiter
*The six-cylinder engine **revs** freely. When the rpm reach 6,400, an electronic rev limiter takes control to prevent excessively high revs.*

Front-hinged bonnet
Before the 1990s the bonnet on most BMWs opened near the car's front windscreen and was hinged at the front end of the car. Today the bonnet on most BMWs opens at the front and is hinged near the car's front windscreen.

The canvas top on the 325i Cabriolet has to be taken down by hand, but it is easy to do. There are Teflon inserts on all the hinges. They make folding and unfolding very smooth.

BMW built many new extras into the 325i Cabriolet. They included a hidden tool kit. The tools were made especially for use on the 325i Cabriolet.

Strengthened windscreen
Because the 325i Cabriolet is a convertible, it was given a steel-enforced frame around the front windscreen. This is a safety feature designed to protect the driver if the car rolls over.

Smooth braking

Large-vented **disc brakes** on the front wheels make for smooth stops, even at high speeds.

Hidden top

When down, the Cabriolet's canvas top hides away under a metal cover.

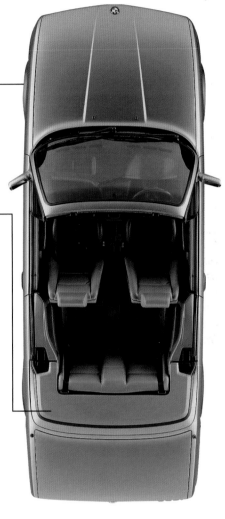

Disc brakes	A type of brake with a rotating disc inside the wheel mechanism. A clip pinches the discs to stop the wheels.
Revs	Short for single revolutions or cycle of a car's engine.

BMW 5 Series

Today one of the world's outstanding cars, BMW's 5 Series was for years overshadowed by the lighter, more nimble 3 Series. That changed dramatically in the 1990s. BMW added a powerful V8 engine to the 5 Series. The whole range was redesigned to make the car sleeker and more **aerodynamic**. Now the main rival to Mercedes-Benz's mid-sized sports saloons, the BMW 5 Series combines luxury with high performance.

Milestones

1972

The 5 Series is introduced. It is the first midsized BMW saloon in a decade.

1983

The 525e — the 'e' stands for *efficiency* — prioritizes better fuel performance over power.

1993

A V8 engine is added to the 540i. It makes the car one of the fastest saloons anywhere.

1996

A revised 5 Series includes a longer *wheelbase* and six-speed transmission.

Vital Statistics for the 1998 BMW 540i	
Top speed:	*220 km/h (137 mph)*
0–60 mph:	*6.11 seconds*
Engine:	*V8*
Engine size:	*4,398 cc (268.4 ci)*
Power:	*286 bhp at 5,700 rpm*
Weight:	*1,680 kg (3,704 lb)*
Fuel economy:	*26 mpg*

There are air bags under the leather and panelling inside the car. They are designed to protect the driver and passengers if the car crashes.

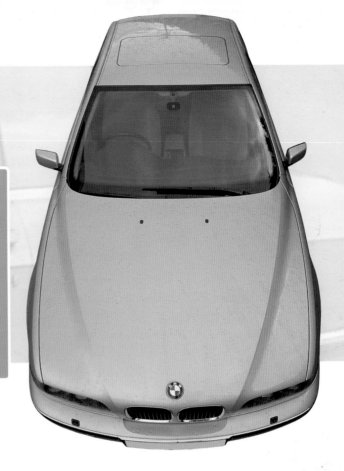

> *"Despite the V8 engine adding weight over the front wheels, the BMW's handling is excellent and the roadholding impressive."*

The early generation 5 Series were much taller and more square than the current models. They did not perform well when turning corners at high speeds. The newer models are more aerodynamic. That makes them better at holding the road.

Aerodynamic   Designed to pass smoothly through the air.

Wheelbase   The distance between the front and back axles.

Specifications

BMW took years of research to develop the 5 Series. The result was a car that was larger and more aerodynamic than the previous model. The 5 Series includes an alloy V8 engine, aluminium suspension and state-of-the-art controls.

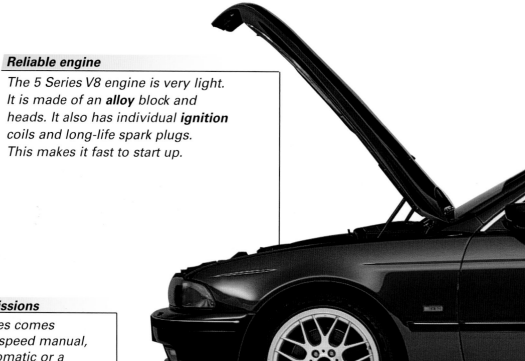

Reliable engine

The 5 Series V8 engine is very light. It is made of an **alloy** block and heads. It also has individual **ignition** coils and long-life spark plugs. This makes it fast to start up.

Different transmissions

The BMW 5 Series comes with either a six-speed manual, a five-speed automatic or a Steptronic (manual but without a clutch) transmission.

 A large amount of the 5 Series is made out of high-strength steel. Steel makes the model 80 per cent more rigid and less prone to bending than previous BMWs.

 Unlike many other engines, the 5 Series V8 engine does not require high revs to gain maximum power.

Lightweight suspension

The 540i has an aluminium suspension to keep the car as light as possible.

Rear sensor

The 540i has a park-distance radar that warns the driver when the vehicle is too close to an obstacle at the rear.

Alloy	A strong but lightweight metal made by mixing other metals.
Ignition	The system that starts the engine of a car.

BMW 750i

The BMW 750i combines sophistication with power. Many people think that it is one of the world's great luxury cars. The 750i is plush and packed with high-tech equipment. It also carries BMW's most powerful engine, the V12. The car is several hundred kilos heavier than its nearest rivals, the Daimler Double Six and the Audi V8 Quattro, but it can accelerate from 0 to 97 km/h (60 mph) a fraction of a second quicker than either of them.

Milestones

1987

The V12 engine is included in the 7 Series range. The car's transmission is *automatic*.

1989

For the first time BMW introduces a short-wheelbase version of the 7 Series.

1996

A 750i is made with Steptronic transmission. Side air bags are added to the 7 Series.

1997

James Bond drives the BMW 750i in the film *Tomorrow Never Dies*.

Vital Statistics for the 1998 BMW 750i L

Top speed:	*249 km/h (155 mph)*
0–60 mph:	*6.5 seconds*
Engine:	*V12*
Engine size:	*5,379 cc (328.2 ci)*
Power:	*322 bhp at 5,000 rpm*
Weight:	*2,065 kg (4,553 lb)*
Fuel economy:	*18.8 mpg*

The interior of the 750i is both luxurious and full of high-tech gadgets. They include a satellite-directed navigation screen.

"The 750i has the agility, poise and handling of a much smaller car. It combines all that with the smooth quietness of the V12."

The massively powerful V12 engine has been used since 1987 in the 7 Series models and in BMW's stylish 8-Series coupe. BMW spent years of development and research on the V12 engine to make it both lightweight and efficient.

Automatic   A car that changes gear automatically.

Specifications

From satellite-monitored navigation to electronically controlled shock absorbers, the 750i is one of the most technically advanced cars on the road. It is also one of the safest, providing front and side air bags to protect the driver and passengers.

Powerful V12

*The all-alloy V12 proved so powerful and efficient in the 750i that BMW adapted the engine for use by the McLaren Formula 1 racing team. The 750i V12 produces 320 **bhp**. The Formula 1 version has an output twice as powerful.*

Adjustable shocks

*Electronically controlled **shocks** make the 750i ride like a much smaller car.*

Automatic tilting mirrors

The 750i's side mirrors tilt down automatically when the car is reversing. They allow the driver to see the kerb and any obstacles on the ground.

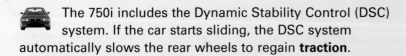

The 750i includes the Dynamic Stability Control (DSC) system. If the car starts sliding, the DSC system automatically slows the rear wheels to regain **traction**.

As with all top-range BMWs, the 750i includes a satellite-controlled navigation system. The system displays directions for the driver on a small screen.

Large boot

The boot of the 750i is very deep and has lots of room. Fitting in big suitcases is no problem.

bhp	Abbreviation for 'brake horsepower', a measurement of an engine's power.
Shocks	Short for 'shock absorbers', devices that smooth out a bumpy ride.
Traction	The grip between a tyre and the surface of the road.

BMW Z3

The Z3 handles well, is powerful and provides excellent **fuel economy**. It is one of the most popular upmarket sports convertibles on the road. The Z3 has a modern look, but it also has nostalgic touches from past sports cars, such as BMW's classic 507. The Z3 is available with either a 1.9- or a 2.8-litre engine. The most powerful version is the M Roadster, which combines the Z3 body with BMW's top-range Motorsport engine.

Vital Statistics for the 1997 BMW Z3

Top speed:	*16.7 km/h (116 mph)*
0–60 m.p.h.:	*8.2 seconds*
Engine:	*In-line four*
Engine size:	*1,895 cc (115.6 ci)*
Power:	*138 bhp at 6,000 rpm*
Weight:	*1,235 kg (2,723 lb)*
Fuel economy:	*29.4 mpg*

The interior setup in the Z3 is similar to that in BMW's other 3 Series cars, but the experience of driving the Z3 is like nothing else.

Milestones

1955

BMW introduces its first post-war sports car, the 507. Too expensive, it sells poorly.

1995

The first Z3 cars are made in BMW's factory at Spartanburg, South Carolina.

1996

A 2.8-litre engine is made optional for the Z3, over-powering the original 1.9.

1997

The M Roadster goes into production. It combines the Z3 body with the M3 engine.

"*There can't be many sports cars easier to drive fast than the tiny Z3.... Even when travelling beyond 160 km/h (100 mph), the Z3 feels rock steady and as solid as a saloon.*"

The BMW 507, made in the 1950s, influenced the design of the Z3. Although now a design classic, the 507 was too expensive at the time it was introduced. It did not sell well. The Z3 has enjoyed a far wider appeal and popularity. This is partly because there are now more drivers who can afford to pay more for a sporty convertible.

Fuel economy How many miles a car can travel on a gallon of petrol.

Specifications

The basic Z3, with a 1.9-litre engine, performs well against the Alfa Romeo Spider. When the engine is boosted to a 2.8-litre or to the M Roadster range, BMW's sports car challenges the Mercedes Benz SLK 230 and the Porsche Boxster.

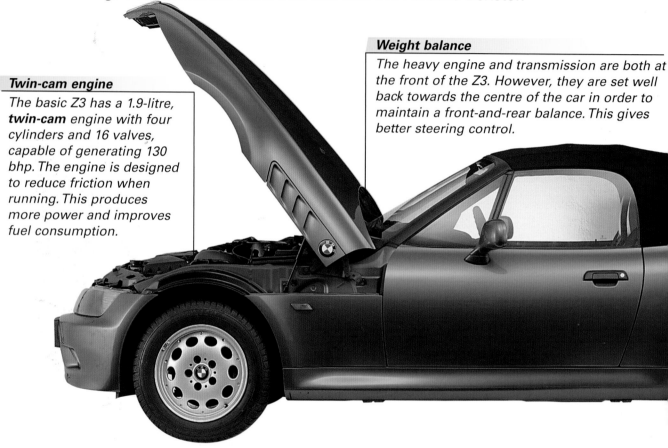

Twin-cam engine

The basic Z3 has a 1.9-litre, **twin-cam** engine with four cylinders and 16 valves, capable of generating 130 bhp. The engine is designed to reduce friction when running. This produces more power and improves fuel consumption.

Weight balance

The heavy engine and transmission are both at the front of the Z3. However, they are set well back towards the centre of the car in order to maintain a front-and-rear balance. This gives better steering control.

The external body panels of the Z3 are bolted in place. On most cars body panels are welded together. Using bolts makes it easier to replace damaged panels.

The side **vents** in the Z3 are more for looks than for performance. Their design is based on the vents on BMW's highly admired 507 sports convertible of the 1950s.

Windscreen columns

The windscreen columns in the Z3 are designed with safety in mind. Reinforced with steel, the windscreen columns are extra thick and strong in order to keep them from buckling if the car overturns.

Long wheelbase

The wheelbase in the Z3 is very long for a small sports car. The long wheelbase minimizes the overhang at the front and rear of the body. This helps to give the Z3 better handling and roadholding.

Wheel options

Although steel wheels are standard in the basic Z3, lightweight alloy wheels are available in the more expensive models.

Twin-cam	An engine with two camshafts, which rotate to open and close the engine's cylinder valves.
Vents	Openings that allow exhaust fumes to escape.

BMW M Series

The 'M' in M Series stands for 'Motorsport'. The range includes the M3 coupé, M5 saloon, the roomy two-door M6 and the M Roadster convertible. All the cars in the M Series are powerful. The first model was the M1. Introduced in 1978, it was in production for only three years. It looked more like a race car than a road car. The M1 had a top speed of 261 km/h (162 mph). Later models in the M Series included the M3 and the M5.

Vital Statistics for the 1990 BMW M5	
Top speed:	*249 km/h (155 mph)*
0–60 mph:	*6.5 seconds*
Engine:	*In-line six*
Engine size:	*3,535 cc (215.7 ci)*
Power:	*310 bhp at 6,900 rpm*
Weight:	*1,725 kg (3,804 lb)*
Fuel economy:	*16 mpg*

Milestones

1978

BMW launches the M1. Inside and out, it is more race car than road car.

1985

The M5 is launched. It is still in production today. The coupé M6, however, only lasted from 1986 to 1989.

1994

The M3 is introduced in the USA.

1997

BMW's powerful and sporty M Roadster becomes available in North America.

The fine leather seats and sporty interior of the M5 are typical of the M Series range.

*"The M3 is one of the finest sport coupés available, with a blend of speed, predictable **rear-wheel drive** handling and practicality that is amazing."*

The M Roadster has the look of the Z3 and the power of the M Series engine. The top speed of the American version of the M Roadster is 220.5 km/h (137 mph). In Europe, where cars are allowed to go faster, the M Roadster can reach up to 249.4 km/h (155 mph).

Rear-wheel drive   A car in which the engine drives the rear wheels.

Specifications

One of the classic examples of the M Series is the M5. In the 1990s, the M5 was a popular choice for upmarket sporty saloons. With Motorsport engineering and power, the M5 performed better than the Audi V8 Quattro and the Lexus LS400.

Front-hinged bonnet

Most modern BMWs have bonnets that open at the front end of the car. However, the M5 kept the traditional front-hinged bonnet.

The engine

The M5 engine has been designed for power and efficiency. It can reach revolutions per minute (rpm) of near 7,000.

Cool brakes

The M5 wheels have very large brakes. To stop them overheating, the wheels have a rotor blade that fans the air to cool the brakes.

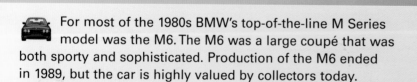

 For most of the 1980s BMW's top-of-the-line M Series model was the M6. The M6 was a large coupé that was both sporty and sophisticated. Production of the M6 ended in 1989, but the car is highly valued by collectors today.

 BMW's marketing department refers to the M3 as one of "the ultimate driving machines."

Strut front suspension

*The M5 has a specially designed front **suspension**. It includes a strut with lower control arms and an anti-roll bar.*

Side mirrors

The side mirrors
can fold in when
the car is parked.

M Series logo

The M Series logo is made up
of three coloured stripes, one
purple, one blue and one red.

Rear spoiler

The rear spoiler (or
aerofoil) makes the
car more stable
at high speeds.

Suspension A system of springs that
support a car and make it
travel more smoothly.

Glossary

aerodynamic: *Designed to pass smoothly through the air.*

alloy: *A strong but lightweight metal made by mixing other metals.*

bhp: *Short for 'brake horsepower', a measurement of an engine's power.*

disc brakes: *A type of brake with a rotating disc inside the wheel mechanism. A clip pinches the disc to stop the wheel.*

fuel economy: *How much petrol a car uses over a certain distance, such as miles per gallon.*

ignition: *The system that starts the engine of a car.*

revs: *Short for single revolutions or cycle of a car's engine.*

roadholding: *A car's ability to grip the road without sliding.*

shocks: *'Shock absorbers', devices that smooth out a bumpy ride.*

suspension: *A system of springs that supports a car and makes it travel more smoothly.*

traction: *The grip between a tyre and the surface of the road.*

transmission: *Speed-changing gears and other parts (such as the drive shaft) that transmit power from engine to wheels.*

twin-cam: *An engine with two camshafts, which open and close the engine's cylinder valves.*

wheelbase: *The distance between the front and back axles.*

Further information

web sites

www.bmw.co.uk/
BMW Great Britain

www.bmw.williamsf1.com
BMW-Williams Formula 1 Team

www.bmwclubs.asn.au/sa/history.html
History of the BMW Motor Company

http://auto.howstuffworks.com/engine.htm
How Stuff Works: Car Engines

books

● Beck, Paul. **Uncover a Race Car: An Uncover It Book.** Silver Dolphin Books, 2003.

● BMW Club of America. **BMW Enthusiast's Companion.** Robert Bentley Publishers, 2003.

● Kiley, Mark. **Inside BMW, The Most Admired Car Company in the World.** John Wiley & Sons Inc., 2004.

● Larimer, Fred. **BMW Buyer's Guide.** Motorbooks International, 2002.

Index

A
aerodynamic 14–16
air bag 14, 18, 20
alloy 16, 17, 20, 25
Alpha Romeo Spider
    24
anti-roll bar 8, 28
Audi A4 Quattro 6
Audi Cabriolet 10
Audi V8 Quattro 18,
    28
axle 9, 15

B
badge 4, 29
Bond, James
    (character) 18

C
convertible 5, 7,
    10–12, 22–24, 26
coupé 6, 10, 11, 19,
    26–28

D
Daimler Double Six 8
disc brakes 7, 13
Dynamic Stability
    Control 20

E
8 Series coupé 19
engine 4, 9, 10, 13, 17,
    20, 21, 25, 27

F
5 Series 5, 14–17
507 22–24
Formula 1 20
front-hinged bonnet
    12, 28
fuel economy 22, 23

L
Lexus LS400 28
logo (*see* badge)

M
Mazda Millennia 6
Mercedes-Benz 14, 24
M5 engine 28
mirrors, side 20, 29
motorcycles 4, 5
Motorsport 4, 22, 26,
    28
M Roadster 5, 22, 24,
    26, 27
M Series 5, 26–29
M Series engine 5, 22,
    27, 28
M3 engine 22

P
park-distance radar
    17
Porsche Boxster 24

R
rear-wheel drive 27
roadholding 10, 11,
    15, 25

S
Saab 900 Turbo 10
saloon 5, 8, 9, 14, 23,
    26, 28
sensors 9, 17
750i 5, 18–21
shock absorbers 8,
    20, 21
six-cylinder engine 6,
    8, 12
spark plugs 16
spoiler (aerofoil) 29

Steptronic 16, 18
suitcases 21
suspension 8, 16, 28,
    29

T
Teflon hinges 12
318i 6
3 Series 5–12, 14, 22
325i Cabriolet 5,
    10–13
Tomorrow Never Dies
    (film) 18
tool kit 12
transmission 8, 9, 14,
    24
twin-cam engine 24,
    25
2.8-litre engine 22

V
V8 engine 14–16
vents 24, 25
V12 engine 18, 19

W
wheelbase 14, 15, 18,
    25
windscreen 9–12, 24

Z
Z3 5, 22–25, 27